Frisky Ducks & Other Poems

Mario Relich

**INTRODUCTION & DRAWINGS
by TOM HUBBARD**

Grace Note
Publications

Frisky Ducks & Other Poems

This edition published 2014 by
Grace Note Publications C.I.C.
Grange of Locherlour,
Ochtertyre, PH7 4JS,
Scotland

books@gracenotereading.co.uk
www.gracenotepublications.co.uk

ISBN 978-1-907676-51-2

First published in 2014

Copyright © Mario Relich 2014
Introduction & Drawings © Tom Hubbard 2014

The right of Mario Relich to be identified as the proprietor of this work has been asserted by him in accordance with the Copyright, Designs and Patents Act 1988

ALL RIGHTS RESERVED
No part of this book may be reproduced in any manner whatsoever, without express written permission from the publisher, except in the case of brief quotations embodied in critical articles and reviews.

A catalogue record for this book is available
from the British Library

Cover designed by Grace Note Publications.

for Wanda, David, and Bridget

Contents

Acknowledgements ... i
Mario Relich: a Generous Wariness
　by Tom Hubbard ... iii

PROLOGUE

Frisky Ducks ... 3

I

Saint Francis ... 6
Cormorant ... 7
Bukowski's Sparrows ... 9
Magpie ... 10
A Fleet of Mallards ... 12
Jubilee 2012 ... 13
Hovering Sparrow ... 14

II

Caruso ... 16
Beloved Infidel ... 19
Old Pontiac: Rawdon Rapids, Quebec ... 21
Mr Hood ... 22
A Soviet Veteran ... 24
Isaac Bashevis Singer ... 27
The Pocket-Diary ... 29

III

A Newgate Portrait ... 32
An Old Woman Cooking Eggs ... 34
Gauguin ... 37
Bomberg's Blackbird ... 38
John Grierson ... 41
Fashion Shoot ... 42
Art Critic ... 43

IV

Just a Thought ... 46
Words and Looks ... 48

	Translator/Traitor	50
	Twilight of a Bibliophile	51
	Godfather	52
	Koan	54
	Heartache	55
V		
	Philosopher on Safari	58
	Grandfather Clock	60
	Losers	62
	Covenant	63
	A Good Man	65
	Siegfried	67
	Talking About Gulls	69
VI		
	The Pianist	72
	Great War Poker	74
	Franco at Bay	76
	Algiers, 1943	77
	Sermon on the Mound	78
	The Only Spanish General in Havana	80
	Air Strike	82
VII		
	Style is the Man	86
	Resurrection	87
	Kingdoms of the Mind	88
	Dragon Fruit	90
	Soap	92
	Ravel's Waltz	93
	Hartford Harmonium	95
EPILOGUE		
	Newton's God	99
	Notes on the Poems	101
	About the Poet	105
	About the Artist	106

Acknowledgements

Some of the poems, or earlier versions of them, have appeared in the following periodicals: *Southlight, Fras, Northwords Now, The Interpreter's House, The Antigonish Review, Chapman, Markings, Lines Review* and *Littack*. Dates of publication are indicated in the Notes. My thanks to all the respective editors.

I am also grateful to my Open University colleagues Evelyn Laidlaw, Elaine Moohan, Lilian Porch and Bob Wilkinson for giving me the opportunity to read some of my poems at an Arts Faculty Conference held at the New Lanark Mill Hotel in September 2012, and to Henry Marsh and Tessa Ransford for inviting me to read at a 'Poetry and Coffee' session in Henderson's Restaurant, Edinburgh, in May 2013.

For valuable advice and discussion on the art and craft of poetry, I would particularly like to thank Vicki Feaver, Elspeth Brown and Kate Hendry, as well as Christine De Luca, Bashabi Fraser, Susan Kreitman, Angela McSeveney and Hushang Philsooph. Their views on poets and poetry have been continually enriching.

I would also like to thank all those who provided encouragement, comments, and unstinting support, but especially Eberhard Bort, for his assistance with editing the manuscript, Joyce Caplan, friend and colleague as Chair of the Poetry Association of Scotland, and Tom Hubbard for his valuable contributions in the presentation of this collection.

Other supportive friends I would like to mention are Frank and Norma Birbalsingh, Ian and Judy Budge, Henry and Sandra Cowper, Malcolm Cox, Roy Dalgleish, Genevieve Glazier, Isobel and John Lodge, Carla Sassi, Harry Smart, Judith Statt, and Alex and Vera Stratton. Special thanks are also due my retired Open University colleagues Ian Donnachie and Tony Aldgate.

Last, but decidedly not least, I owe a lot to my family and to friends, some of whom are mentioned in the dedications to some of the poems.

MARIO RELICH: A GENEROUS WARINESS

by Tom Hubbard

It must have been sometime in the mid-1980s, shortly after I started work at the Scottish Poetry Library, that I came across the name Mario Relich. At that time one of my tasks was to sort through back issues of Scottish cultural magazines, and the strange name would crop up in *Scottish International*; I had remembered that as a much talked-about publication up in Aberdeen, where I had been a student during the previous decade. Although Aberdeen was its own intellectual and academic centre, from time to time various Edinburgh luminaries would appear at teach-ins (very much 1960s/1970s phenomena), and an especially kenspeckle figure was Hamish Henderson, who would take part in the northern city's literary-political events and who could be heard in the English department, asking for the whereabouts of his old friend, the eminent Burns scholar Tom Crawford. At such times Aberdeen pubs like Ma Cameron's or the Prince of Wales would take on a bit of the ambience of Milnes or the Abbotsford.

However, I never encountered the mysterious Mario Relich there and then, nor indeed until well into the '80s, by which time I was reading his reviews of Edinburgh Festival events in *The Scotsman*. The founding director of the Scottish Poetry Library, Tessa Ransford, had taken over the editorship of *Lines Review*, and Mario was appearing in its pages as a book reviewer. I wasn't aware of him as a poet – indeed, not unlike his Open University colleague Angus Calder (who is fondly remembered in the following pages), Mario kept his own poetry under wraps for a long time. As happens, the secret eventually came out, and now it is here before us, and for the first time as a book.

For much of the 1990s I was working abroad, but I had a Scottish interregnum in the middle of the decade, and I think our first seriously friendly encounter was in a pub just after the funeral of the poet Tom Scott. We were in the company of Angus Calder who had his quiet way of making consequential introductions. I was back from the US in 1998, undergoing reverse culture shock and looking (as now) for scraps of paid work. Mario, who was at that time teaching part-time in the Humanities Department of Edinburgh College of Art, urged me to do likewise. As colleagues at ECA for a couple of years we saw much of each other, and it was a fitting location to enjoy conversations about the visual arts – including cinema – as well as literature. I regard Mario as a mentor when it comes to questions of film (noting, in the present context, his poem about John Grierson); and indeed I still feel awe when I consider that he was writing for the capital's cultural magazines over forty years ago when I was still an undergraduate from provincial Fife.

There is nothing provincial about the poems in this collection. Local at times, yes, with evocations of the poet's various home bases, but as the likes of William Carlos Williams and Patrick Kavanagh would remind us, the local is the universal. Mario Relich is of Croatian and Italian parentage, and he grew up in Canada; Edinburgh has been his home for much of his working life, though there have been teaching stints with adult education classes at the University of Hull in Scarborough and at Goldsmiths College, University of London. His work with the Open University means that he often has to be on the move, but Edinburgh always reclaims him.

The poems are deceptively low-key: he pays you, the reader, a compliment by tacitly inviting you to interpret his silences. The short lines succeed each other in their unassuming way, then he delivers a sudden charge, right at the end: take, for example, 'Caruso', or 'Philosopher on Safari'. Mario Relich can deal with shocking subjects and yet maintain what Robert Louis Stevenson would call an 'old-world charm'. This poet is of both the Old World and the New, intensely European in his range of cultural references, but also transatlantic, whether evoking family and university life in Montreal or verbally transcribing, as it were, a postcard depicting the Civil War memorial in Hartford, Connecticut, and linking this with that city's poet Wallace Stevens, himself redolent of European imagination and American experience. The two worlds clash, though, if sadly and poignantly, in the Caruso poem noted above: the poet's mother, uprooted from her native Italy, can never feel entirely at home in Canada.

It's chiefly in the poems about birds – one type, of course, is the source of the book's title – that we witness, in Muriel Spark's phrase, 'the transfiguration of the commonplace'. Again, it's that quiet way of discovering the miraculous in the ordinary. There is no straining after inflated significance: the hovering sparrow resists comparison with Vaughan Williams's lark ascending, but we're genially invited to consider a reference to the New Testament. Then there is the cormorant, so rarely seen by the Union Canal in Edinburgh, but there it is after all, grandly Ovidian: nature and culture thus brought together, but without fuss.

Likewise, Mario Relich has a knack of wry aversion to all that is shallow and crass in contemporary Western society, as in 'Losers' or 'Fashion Shoot', the latter more genuinely feminist than many a self-righteous (and self-serving) theoretical campus diatribe. It's better to be dead-pan than po-faced. As a university teacher, Dr Relich knows only too well just how obscurantist the fetishisation of critical theory has become. He has occasionally written under the pseudonym of Henry Ryecroft, a name borrowed from the semi-autobiographical 'private papers' composed by the novelist George Gissing (1857-1903), the chronicler there (and in *New Grub Street*, 1891) of down-at-heels literary folk struggling to maintain cultural values in the careerist hack-world of late Victorian Britain. 'Even the best editions of our day', writes Gissing's Ryecroft, 'have so much of the mere school-book; you feel so often that the man does not regard his author as literature, but simply as text. Pedant for pedant, the old is better than the new.' I can imagine Mario Relich saying amen to that. His literary loyalties are deeper and more expansive, as in his barely-concealed excitement at the memory of Isaac Bashevis Singer's 1968 lecture at Montreal's McGill University: the poet's east-central European affinities with Singer come through surely and strongly. The lecturer is passionate in discussing *Anna Karenina*, while maintaining 'a goblin-like twinkle in his eyes'.

Is there something old-fashioned as well as old-world about all this? Probably. I know that Mario doesn't care to order books over the internet, preferring the traditional way of happy chance finds in the second-hand bookshops (or their New World equivalents, used bookstores). Again, this is very Henry Ryecroft-like: he'll warm to the Gissingesque choice between buying a coveted book (thus going hungry for the day), or foregoing the literary treat and spending his scant coin on a meal, and of course opting for the former course – as against some academic bureaucrat taking everything for granted on a six-figure salary while imposing cuts on the chalk-face minions. But it must be added that Mario is a man of enlightened opinions and would be averse to Gissing's/Ryecroft's more curmudgeonly and even reactionary pronouncements.

As for other discoveries in this collection, set his citation of a Croat folk proverb beside the traditionally Scottish nature of his 'bird' poems – that is to say, the line of fable-poetry from Henryson through Soutar and beyond. We don't often witness the coalescence of the laconic and the romantic, but we have it here in his portrait of a Montreal worthy in 'Mr Hood'. Ironic juxtapositions are rarely far away: the family goes for a ride in the Pontiac car of 1950s Canada, but what about these forests redolent of the Iriquois and the original Pontiac, the warrior-chief of Francis Parkman's bio-history?

Then there is Wagner's *Ring*, the vast music-drama succinctly rendered with Siegfried, its hero, worn down and destroyed by the pettiness of those around him. We encounter another musical reference with 'Ravel's Waltz', on that piece which initially promises a southern-French pastiche of Viennese *Gemütlichkeit* but metamorphoses into a *danse macabre* for a post-1914 Europe.

And yet Mario Relich can be joyously celebratory of nature – especially of his birds – as against the more gratuitously tenebrous irruptions of the human. 'A Fleet of Mallards' is on the side of the exhilaration he feels in contemplating avian life at its liveliest. He sets this against a piece of nearby graffiti – 'The World Owes You Nothing'. The growly small-mindedness of that utterance reminds us of much that is repellent in Scotland, or as the late poet Alan Bold puts it, the 'Land of the Omnipotent No'. I think Mario would have relished the more imaginative graffiti I saw in a Budapest underpass: 'One atom bomb is enough to ruin your whole day.' Mario Relich's vision is a wary one, but it's also generous. Moreover, Baudelaire (of whom both Mario and I are avid students) maintained that a poem could also serve as a piece of art criticism; Mario Relich, friend of all the arts, supplies at once poetry and percipience on painters as diverse as Velasquez, Gauguin and David Bomberg.

Fife 2014

PROLOGUE

... every good poem is very nearly a utopia...

from *The Dyer's Hand and Other Essays*

W H Auden

FRISKY DUCKS

Raindrops splashed into the Canal,
while drakes and ducks bobbed along,
oblivious to the stormy gusts of wind,
some beginning to flap their wings.

As I walked along, some flew away,
while I watched them, feeling wetter,
nearly soaked through my winter coat,
and my glasses misting with drizzle.

For these birds it was just a time
to be frisky, drakes flirting with ducks,
even if I mainly heard the wind
and the rain, which splashed on me.

It wasn't really a matter of 'the rain, it
raineth every day,' but more a glimpse
of how the rain might be very remote
from revealing what we really feel.

I

... Then when least expected there appears
a pair of duck shooters, discordant in their relation
to land and water ...

from The Duck Shooters

Stewart Conn

SAINT FRANCIS

ditch mobile
kill walkman

I see a blackbird
build her nest
another, on patrol

oh yes, freedom
in your head
not in trainers

you jog
if you want
I won't

CORMORANT

      for David and Hildegard Smart

I walked via the canal
to town the other day
a cold, wintry one,
surprised by seeing
a rare visitor, who
just didn't belong
with the mallards here:
a wonderfully graceful
ducking and diving
sort of large, solitary
waterfowl, with a hooked
beak, its ancestry
quite reptilian.

It dived and disappeared
and then, after suspenseful
seconds, appeared again,
and did so repeatedly,
its black head resurfacing,
like a periscope,
where I least expected it.

It took me a while
before I realised,
so utterly strange
it looked, that its
identity was not
that of a different
duck but a cormorant,
a bird, and this one
of royal lineage
so we are told by Ovid,
you just about
never see anywhere
near the city canal.

*Charles Bukowski
1920–1994*

BUKOWSKI'S SPARROWS

There they are,
pecking away
at birdseed
hanging low
in our garden:

sparrows,
shades of brown,
but one male
more enticing,
a shinier tint.

A female
watches him,
getting more
than the others,
and gets near him.

Or so I imagine
while reading
Bukowski,
his poems
so plain.

It's not always
a matter
of bright colours,
just the mundane
ticking along.

MAGPIE

> *If a magpie chatters in a high tree or building, guests are coming. If a magpie chatters from down low, there will be hell.*
> Croat folk saying

It wasn't quite
like The Texas
Chainsaw Massacre,
just an excruciating,
scraping noise, it
seemed to come
from a joiner nearby,
perhaps fixing
a window.

But all I could see
was a tree, its leaves
shimmering green.
I looked up, and there
it was, what I'd heard
was the harsh,
brazen squawk
of a lone magpie.

It perched completely
rigid, as if frozen, not
at all lively like the
thieving magpie of
Rossini's happy opera.

It reminded me more,
if only momentarily,
of Kubrick's film
A Clockwork Orange,
in which the music was
speeded up to highlight
the brutal humour
of futuristic thugs
beating up a shabby,
alcoholic old tramp.

But this magpie
had nothing fierce
or lethal about it,
nor anything to laugh
about. The split-
second timing
of its mimicry, so
much like deliberate
mischief, was simply
startling, that's all.

All I could do
was walk away,
and shrug my
shoulders. It
started again, lower
down this time,
a bird of ill omen,
folklore tells us,
this one intent,
if I linger too long,
on giving me
a migraine.

A FLEET OF MALLARDS

Under the bridge
I spied some mallards,
preparing to land,
with some already
splashing about,
while on the other side
of the canal bank
I glimpsed this graffiti
warning: THE WORLD
OWES YOU NOTHING.

But watching closely
these blue-streaked
drakes having
a raucous time, fit
and ready to pursue
and fight over females,
amused and on alert
for them, that's one
way of shrugging off
an indifferent world.

JUBILEE 2012

      Union Canal, Edinburgh

Walking by the canal
I saw the mallards
who chased each other
in riotous competition.

Disdainful females
quacking back,
sparked the thought
that none of them really

cared if they were here
in Scotland or further south,
equally at home so near
the city, or in the country.

Delivered in sonorous
quacks, their allegiance
owed nothing to a great,
omnipotent sky-drake

they dared not cross,
nor an elder preening
with hereditary authority:
they merely followed

their urges. Deference
was only grudgingly
yielded to the strongest
of their rowdy breed.

HOVERING SPARROW

What is it about
a sparrow as it
hovers in the air,
a static whirr?

The canal below
the bird sparkles
with sun-rays rippling
in the placid water.

It's not like Vaughan
Williams, his Lark
Ascending so ecstatic
on tremulous violin.

Quickly, helter-skelter,
it lands and hides
in a cluster of Bishop's
Weed which sways

in mild abandon.
Just a blur at first,
but take a look at
the New Testament:

a sparrow even when
it falls, we are told,
is divinely protected,
that's why if no blithe

spirit like the skylark,
what it does do is hover
as if in a state of bliss,
yet so very briefly.

II

Thus, costumed images before me pass,
Haunting your archives architectural:
Coureur de bois, in posts where pelts were portaged;
Seigneur within his candled manoir; Scot
Ambulant through his bank, pillar'd and vast.

from 'Montreal'

A. M. Klein

CARUSO

My mother was really
keen on Mario Lanza.

On a snow-bound day,
she took me to the local

cinema to see
The Great Caruso,

an MGM film
spectacularly grand,

the lion roaring
at its start, a movie

colourful and operatic,
the women glamorous.

A love story beat
at its heart, the tenor

a troubled, unhappy man
I couldn't fathom. It was

no doubt a typical
Hollywood biopic

of the time. I felt
my mother's warmth

in the dark. I couldn't
have been much more

than seven or eight,
so I was thrilled

to do something
so very grown-up.

watching with her Lanza
singing passionately

heartfelt arias, like
the one from *Tosca*,

his voice breaking
into stirring sobs

which I found alarming,
even overwhelming.

At the final scene,
he collapsed on stage,

and shocked silence
gripped everyone.

The cinema curtain
as if on mournful cue

shrouded the screen
announcing THE END.

'If only I could take
you to *La Scala*,

in Milano, so plush,
so luxurious, yes

you'd like it, I think so,
but there are no opera

houses here,'
sighed my mother.

'What's an opera
house?,' I wondered,

having no inkling
that Montreal

was not home to her,
and never would be.

BELOVED INFIDEL

OK, it was just
Hollywood hokum,
a melodrama about
a washed-up writer
and his final fling
in an alcoholic haze.

But what struck me
was Gregory Peck,
I loved his films
because he looked
a bit melancholy,
sensitive, and dignified,
manly, but neither too
macho, nor effete.

And Deborah Kerr?
I could not wish then
for a sexier woman,
yet not blatantly so,
unlike Marilyn Monroe,
or so I felt, despite
her famous horizontal
clinch with Burt Lancaster,
as the waves surged
over their manic kissing
in *From Here to Eternity*.

So it took me by surprise
that Peck gave her a hard
time, often angry,
or depressed, between
bouts of romantic love-
making, coded as either
riotous scenes of 'having
fun' south of the border,

down Mexico way, or
rapturous kisses
orchestrally amplified.

That what the story
sugared was actually
the failure of F. Scott
Fitzgerald to make it
as a scriptwriter
in Hollywood, a fatal
heart-attack his reward,
the sentimentality of
the romantic love-story
could not disguise.

OLD PONTIAC: RAWDON RAPIDS, QUEBEC

The rapids and the rocks,
the fifties in Canada, Presley
on the car radio switched off,
and I a sullen teen-ager,
even if barely thirteen. My father,
a dour, anti-Communist Croat,
drove an old Pontiac flecked
with traces of rust, and my
mother smiled at my younger
brother and myself, sitting behind.
I had some inkling she yearned
to drive it herself.

Was it really good enough for her,
so Italian in her exuberance,
to be in charge only of our picnic?
She offered us, like a sacrament,
ham on rye bread with plenty
of mustard and gherkins. We
sat on the rocks, the roar of the
falls not as loud as Niagara, but
loud enough for a hush to envelop
us all, as we ate quietly, my brother
visibly bored, and I restless
for adventure.

I looked at the car, fixated
on the sheen of its sky-blue
metal polish, and rear-lights
like sleek rocket fins, daydreaming
of a girlfriend pressing beside me; yet
I could envisage much more vividly,
a lesson from history: Iroquois lurking
behind the greenery of the spruces
and pines surrounding us, warriors
hell-bent in their painted faces
on scalping our entire family, fierce
like the original Pontiac.

MR HOOD

After we grew bored with our little spat
about a lucky horseshoe claimed by us both,
the snag being that only one of us found
this rusted treasure in a rubbish dump,
my brother and I could see from the upper-
floor window of my room, dad talking
to Mr Hood just over the fence.

He had a grizzled, leathery face,
weather-beaten, and yet sunny
in disposition. We knew he was
very old, ninety we were told,
but his stories I always loved.

He talked so much about life
in the forests, a great wilderness,
we liked to think, and not too remote
from the outskirts of our adopted
city, Montreal.

Dad reiterated all the time
to Mr Hood about freedom
and opportunity that he found
in Canada, a refuge from
his iron-curtained homeland.

Mr Hood listened, and maybe
he understood, an old war
at the back of his mind,
but he changed the subject.

It was apples he preferred,
which he grew in his garden,
and he liked to talk about how best
to grow them, giving us some,
very much to mum's delight.

He was a retired tree-surgeon
with the Canadian Forest Service
but we just thought of him
as a lumber-jack, and imagined
that in a distant, adventurous
time, so familiar from westerns.
he wore a chequered, colourful,
heavy-duty shirt we fancied
for ourselves. Or at least I did,
not him, my younger brother,
always more fastidious,
still insists.

Only years later did I hear and
understand all too well, Robert
Frost's poem, which he recited
in a gravelly voice, sounding so
much like old Mr Hood, on why
fences make good neighbours.

A SOVIET VETERAN

>   for Joe and Rachel Garver

As he talked to my brother
and me, we could see
he had at least a couple
of gold teeth.

But what he had to tell us,
reflected nothing at all
like a sunny disposition,
his smile was so brief.

And his sarcasm was like
a sucker punch we didn't
see coming: 'This country
is rotting with too much

liberty. You boys just don't
get what it takes to be a man;
no, I'd better rephrase that,
you've got no self-discipline!'

How could he possibly
be my father's friend?
He'd always warned us
against the Reds.

But this Russian was
actually a defector,
adept at import/export
in his adopted country.

Now a tough New Yorker,
he was the kind of man
successful and respected
in the democratic West.

After all, he drove a tank
at the Battle of Kursk, yet
he hated Communism,
said my father later on.

Looking back,
we were on holiday,
and I knew my mother
wasn't impressed.

I sensed her distaste,
so my brother and I
simply shrugged him off,
to us, much too weird.

Visiting New York,
just a drive away
from our home
in suburban,

English-speaking
Montreal, was very
exciting. We loved
the tall buildings,

skyscrapers straight
out of *King Kong*,
and dancers at Radio
City Music Hall.

It was the autumn
of the Cuban Missile
Crisis, and Kennedy
had perfect teeth.

POLSKA
1.55 ZŁ
NY PARKS DEPARTMENT
DO NOT FEED THE PIGEONS
Hudson River
East River
ISAAC BASHEVIS SINGER
1904
1991

ISAAC BASHEVIS SINGER

It was winter 1968,
or thereabouts, that
Isaac Bashevis Singer,
Yiddish storyteller
and New Yorker,
was guest speaker
at a university Jewish
students' philosophical
society in Montreal.

His topic was Tolstoy
and *Anna Karenina*.
Oddly, looking back,
he addressed a small
audience, with myself
an outsider, one addicted
to Singer's translated
tales of human weakness,
demonic powers, and
false messiahs almost
like pulp fiction, even
if from a vanished world
of the Polish *shtetls*.

But it was panoramic
realists like the great
Russians he admired,
emulating them in one
or two of his own
modern realist novels.

And he was smitten
above all not by Natasha
in *War and Peace*,
but Tolstoy's tormented
heroine in his 'other' great

novel. For Singer, her
suffering was not merely
spiritual, but intensely
sexual, Vronsky,
afflicted by tooth-ache,
in the end much too little
to recognise what her
love really meant.

Singer's talk, delivered
with great passion, and
something of a goblin-like
twinkle in his eyes,
caused a flurry of
consternation, and
angry exchanges.

No one had the slightest
inkling that the Nobel Prize
would be his one day, and
the room in which he spoke
seemed dark, perhaps
dimly lit, but his face shone
with messianic fervour.

Outside, it was a still,
frozen night.

THE POCKET-DIARY

In memoriam David Pirnie

He was greatly
engaged
in conversation
with a woman
friend of his
at the *Scottish
Pen* office.

As I knocked
and came in,
on an errand
I can't recall,
he saw me
checking I had
a date right.

'Do you always
carry such a small
red pocket-diary
with you?,' he said,
smiling, and then
he couldn't help
laughing, so used
was he to his own

weighty *iPad*,
black like a Model T
Ford, but his forte
was complete
empathy, not
the assembly-line
mentality.

III

… The sun
shines on grass. The sun mirrors off my blue. And
earth's smell wafts over. …

from 'The Meadow'

Kurt Schwitters

A NEWGATE PORTRAIT

Oh yes, do paint my rosary
on this bare table:
it's papist I know,
but my only link to God.

And why do I have to look away from you?
You, who are my guest
as I sit pensively serene
in my barred prison cell,
convicted of murder,
and sudden death my fate.

Yet, suppose I did kill my mistress
and her two servants besides.
Well, it's bloody fame for me,
and a bob or two for you!

Still, my head is covered
in a clean white bonnet
and light, yes very shadowy,
shines on my face.

Sure, I am not praying,
no, my arms are folded,
leaning on the table:
a dignified pose O Lord!

And do not forget
my pocket crucifix,
it's not a trinket!

You said yourself
I am 'capable
of any wickedness'.

That's your verdict
about 'this woman's features',
yet you refuse to face me.

But ask yourself:
is my dress really so sooty black?
Look how it billows!
I shall ascend into heaven,
You'll see!

AN OLD WOMAN COOKING EGGS

> I would rather be the first painter of common things, than second in higher art.
> Diego Velazquez

Velazquez reveals
in The Rokeby Venus
the goddess looking
at Cupid's mirror

turned away from us,
but her face looks back
at our eyes, in reflected
distortion, her allure

so powerful. If we turn
to his early painting
An Old Woman Cooking Eggs,
It's the power of the ordinary

which wins out instead
in its play of light
and dark, understated
chiaroscuro at its best.

Look at the young boy
wearing black, almost
satin in texture, like
a knight or hidalgo,

holding firmly, not a lance,
which he would prefer,
but a large, tantalising
melon, its weight

evident in the clutch
of his left hand and
shoulder, so typical
of his humble role

in a genre piece,
which clients at the time
called a mere bodegon.
And look at the woman:

she wears a coarse,
homespun ochre-brown
dress, head and shoulders
covered in linen white

almost like a nun's habit,
while she holds an egg
in her left hand,
and a wooden spoon

on her right, in order
for two eggs to carefully
fry in oil, contained
by a terracota pot.

It's a painting where
we feel confident
that the eggs
will be ready to eat,

and that we need wait
only for the woman
who is briefly looking
to her right at the boy,

perhaps giving him
instructions, hence
his frown, to add
the other egg. She

is so self-contained,
that she dominates
the painting, not the
utensils, as art-critics

and even the painter
so intent on proving
himself claim. Not at
all, his artistic prowess

is so much greater:
it's transparent
that she radiates
beauty through her

strength of character,
unlike Lucian Freud's
Naked Girl with Egg,
so sleepily passive,

her right breast
pendulous; an image fit
for stark desire, the eggs
just an afterthought.

GAUGUIN

       Martinique, 1887

Here I sit
in my hut,
it's a native's,
but what of it,
savage that I am.

Look here,
as I see it,
my dear Mette,
riotous colours
beckon to me.

A cockerel peeks,
nearly lost,
scratching earth,
you can't see him,
not at first.

I can see he's
nothing much,
and neither am I,
hidden like him,
in what I see:

Shrubs and trees,
a mountain peak,
and distant
sea, the sky blue
with a swirl of white.

It's a dazzling vista,
one that moves me,
with mystic fervour,
yet I am no saint,
just myself.

BOMBERG'S BLACKBIRD

for Catherine and Jim Fowler

A blackbird, glimpsed
from our bay-window,
stern like a sentinel,
alert and chirping,
surveyed his territory,
as he perched, a mere
black blur, nearly hidden
on the overgrown hedge.

 It rained lightly, while
we watched on the flat-screen,
safe in our sitting-room,
an earnest, tousle-haired
art-critic singing the praises
of David Bomberg, and
his modernist painting,
The Mud Bath.

With its jagged, steel-like
girders, like bolts of lightning,
and a black, vertical upright
chimney or Moloch,
the zig-zagging girders
red, white, and blue,
like the Union Jack, it's
a pattern all too prophetic.

Its rhythmic abstractions,
we were informed,
resemble swimmers
plunging and diving in
a Whitechapel community
swimming-pool, while others
dry themselves, ostensibly
what Bomberg depicted.

But look again, you'll see,
as the title suggests,
that Shevzik's Vapour Baths
in Brick Lane was nearer
his vision, its mud-treatment
renowned, and reinvigorating
for his barely discernible
towelled figures.

He painted his steely,
yet far from sombre, vision
on the eve of a war which
shattered the lives of millions,
a desolation in which hedges
withered or burned to
acrid smoke, a landscape of
skeletal cinders.

Such a field of mud and ash
we liked to think, was even
here redeemed by hedge-rows,
far enough from trenches,
in which blackbirds
could still build their nests,
oblivious to the pounding
of artillery fire.

Bust of John Grierson (1898-1972)
by Kenny Munro at Stirling Railway Station.

Photo© Kenny Munro

JOHN GRIERSON

Remember the zealous filmmaker
Whose scorn lay in his glance
So beware of looking askance
At the postman's round
And the miner's sweat
Flickers of film in Grierson's eyes
His focal vision aimed for truth
Not the self-indulgent peep-hole trance
Others call a slice of life.

Here, the lyric energy of booming shipyards
Hammering away in documentary montage
Remote from the labyrinths of personal lives
Men at work, not play, or domestic routines.

He recorded a world now vanished
Collectively inspired, but individually hard
Life for many in Britain, at least those in work
Still worse for the workless
Before Big Brother, and Hitler's war
Yet he admired Leni Riefenstahl
Awed by *Triumph of the Will*
That fuehrer-mad fantasy, a crooked lie
In the shape of the swastika
He declared it to be great art
However repugnant the politics.

Documenting the truth when very old
No longer seemed to him so urgent, but *Drifters*
His saga of fishermen steaming to shoals of herring
Still recollects the world of work before the Crash.

FASHION SHOOT

Click away
if you must,
the model
is right in front
of you, and you
could be David
Hemmings in
Blow-Up,
but she's no
Vanessa
Redgrave,
who struck me
as so restless
and delicately
topless.

        Now
all you're doing
is to erase
any trace
of intellect
in a woman's
face, not even
a sultry one,
far less defiant,
just a vacant
stare. It's what
your clients
want, and brand
new accessories
on naked skin.

ART CRITIC

for Sara Lodge

It was in 1945, not long
after the war, that I first
revelled in Paul Klee,
his paintings on show

in the National Gallery,
while daylight streamed
from the windows,
heralding the end

of sirens and air-raids.
But lately, honoured
by seventeen
claustrophobic rooms

for the exhibition
at the Tate Modern,
something of their colour-
coded vibrancy captured

in my memory was lost.
Yet Like a Window Pane,
far from dulled, was
dazzling in its dripping

squares of shimmering
colour. It looked like
an abstract pattern
on stained glass

in a modern cathedral.
Just gauze on cardboard,
but so translucent,
it still made its impact.

A poet as well, he
was much better
known for his
luminous prose,

as in *Pedagogical
Sketchbook*,
where he takes
'a line for a walk.'

The exhibition
I remember is now
long-forgotten, but
a year later, Orwell

wrote: 'Good prose
is like a window pane.'
Klee's art makes us note
how poetic that sounds.

IV

And which of us doesn't occasionally
want one of the old gods to come down
and chase us over the sands?

from 'Oi Yoi Yoi'

Vicki Feaver

JUST A THOUGHT

So, farewell
friends and family,
I fed the birds
and went to bed.

Not quite
like the Stoic
cutting his veins
and taking a bath.

Nero's orders,
how thrilling
to humble
your tutor!

Or the revolver
on the table,
and a glass
of whisky.

Disgrace
was intolerable,
nothing doing
but oblivion.

At heart it's pain
we can't stomach
and fear most,
it's too much.

But we do things
differently now,
just pills
and hey presto,

it's over
and done with,
an undiscovered
country invisible
in the mist.

WORDS AND LOOKS

When the knife
twists slowly
in the flesh

it twists
remorselessly
without mercy

like a man
who cannot sleep
because of pain

pain so dull
that haunting thoughts
he can't escape

yet so sharp
that his thoughts
make no sense.

When the knife
sank beyond survival
in the flesh

revenge was
not really the Lord's
but the wild justice

of a kinsman's duty
in archaic times
less civilised

but is it really better
when words and looks
are the real killers

words and looks
that rankle fiercely
in the mind

yet leave no trace
like cancer dormant
in the flesh?

TRANSLATOR/TRAITOR

No, I am not
a translator,
you say so
led astray by
my accent,
which sounds
so alien to you.

Translators are
traitors, an Italian
witticism has it,
but really that's
so utterly false
about the art
of translation.

Such betrayal
poets find not
at all problematic:
like Judas's kiss,
it was so tragic
yet necessary
for salvation.

But translation,
let me be blunt,
is not my trade:
I write my own
poems, in my
own language,
also yours.

TWILIGHT OF A BIBLIOPHILE

Yes, it will come to pass,
my books will outlive me,
just left to kith and kin,
or donated to Oxfam.

They are so much a part
of myself, and my life
so enriched by authors,
all vital – dead or alive.

Montaigne was my guide
one day, Pascal on another,
Dostoevsky always,
Kafka, Tolstoy favourites.

What a funeral pyre
the books would make!
But then history tells me,
book-burners are killers.

Among the torched,
let me name Brecht
Proust, Rushdie,
and Arundhati Roy.

Their books live on,
I can't be a pyromaniac,
or like Hitler in his bunker,
book-burner cornered,

trapped in petrol-soaked
immolation. All he left
was a testament of hate,
utterly reviled to this day.

GODFATHER

I'm not on Facebook,
and you can't tweet me.

Don't go for e-mail,
it will only ricochet.

Forget about faxing
me, or giving me a call.

There is just no way
you can find me, no

matter what you do,
or how hard you try.

I'll call you, don't
call me, when your

time is up. You'll
know it's all over

because I'll remind
you, and you'll have

nowhere to hide; it's
not that I'll make you

an offer you can't
refuse, it's just not

my style, there is
nothing for you

to decide. I call
the shots, that's all

you can expect.
Look at it this way:

You'll hear from me
in my own good time.

That's a promise,
and it will be kept.

KOAN

You need not wait for death,
Death lies in wait for you.

HEARTACHE

Home is where
your heart is,
but when you're dead,
your heart stops.

You see a forest,
green with life,
turn to desert,
brown and lifeless.

Or a scorching sun
which can't be faced,
just endured.

Yet night must fall,
so find a light,
and look for home.

V

It is bareness I want, the bareness of the knife's blade. And the words to be going away from me like ducks settling on the sea when night is falling, their wings folded on the sea, and the night falling.

from 'Bareness'

Iain Crichton Smith

PHILOSOPHER ON SAFARI

University of Ife, Nigeria, 1977

His face all tanned,
and neatly bearded,
the safari philosopher,
nonchalant, resembling
a languid Edwardian,
polite to his fingertips,
carefully combs his hair
at the steering-wheel.

Beside him in his red
VW converted armoured car,
a girl from Bloomington,
Indiana, her father
an academic on tropical
assignment, wears
an adire-cloth wraparound
Tye-Dye print of geometric lizards
copied from an Escher print.
She looks in the rear-view mirror
and smoothes her hair
so as not to overly dishevel
her pre-Raphaelite look.

One is slightly fluent in Yoruba,
the other very impressed.
Just a dash of it from him
spices up her desire
for Afrocentric stimulation
from the white Englishman.

Or so she thinks
as the sun singles them out
close to the harsh laughter
of all the beer-swillers
under the shade of a mango

stamping on ants
and fiercely discussing
the imminent return
of civilian rule
and the latest toll
of students shot.

GRANDFATHER CLOCK

The clock struck 12,
its stately pendulum
swayed like a scythe.

'Oh no, it's not death,
the hooded one
we fear so much,

even if we're cozy
in the lounge
of this plush hotel;

it's just the force
of gravity swaying
as it ticks,'

so my friend,
wise with cognac,
the white-haired poet,

maths his metier,
words his love,
confided to me.

We met in Bled,
his French accent
elegant and lucid.

He reveled
in proving his point
as he marveled

at such simple
physics so easy
to understand, yet

his anxious look,
too unconvivial
for conference

delegates like us,
betrayed what
he really thought.

LOSERS

'Winners, you've got to believe me,
don't have the *time* to be nice.'
So declared Irving 'Swifty' Lazar,
as Bogart called him, agent

and dealmaker to the Hollywood
greats. He knew all about winners.
'There are only winners and losers,'
said Swifty, 'being a winner is just

a matter of always striking hard.
You don't need to be popular,
and you don't need friends,
but look out for the right kind.

To be frank, you've got to have
what it takes, and don't whine
or sound off if you fail, no one
will listen, just pick yourself up.

Stand alone, like John Wayne, or
even Rambo: Remember, you're
a winner if you think you are,
keep your feet on the ground,

eyes on the stars. You're
a loser if you've got the time
of day, or night, for any jerk
who's just a waste of time.'

But wheeling and dealing
with David Frost, on behalf
of Nixon, the Watergate loser,
he finally met his match.

COVENANT

for Ian and Helen Wood

Church spires
of predestined rigidity
jet-black against the sky
summon the elect,
or what's left of them,
the saving remnant,
to the straight
and narrow path
which ascends
grimly upwards
to the eternal
 reward of the Just.

Unlike the tortuous casuistry
of winding streets leading
to the drunken ribaldry
of sulphurous public cellars
choking with smoke no more,
but still with lewd talk.

And yet
Providence intervenes
as if from the Magdalen Chapel
nearby, promising a Day of Wrath
to come, as the windy wetness
of torrential rains yields reflections
of glancing church spires desecrated
in resilient mud.

The Elect are different now
indifferent to Apocalypse,
if not Austerity,
pursuing stock-market prices,
their early morning ritual

that of cappuccino-gulping
movers and shakers
blissful about nothing but
cellphone ring-tones
on the way to sleek, functional
office-buildings whitened
in the morning sun
and built to challenge the spires
of which Edinburgh was once
precipitously proud.

A GOOD MAN

In memoriam John Brown, Historian, 1937-2012

It wasn't the time of day,
or the weather, drearily
capricious sleet and snow,
the icy lashings of winter,

or the welcome caress
of sunlight in summer,
it didn't matter, the point
for you was plain:

while sipping coffee,
it was to argue, with no
quarter given, or expected,
that was bliss to you,

so long as you won. But
you could not tolerate
complacency, or a shrug
of indifference.

The Welfare State
was your lodestar:
a society ruled
by kindness, not

proceeds of profits
trickling down, or
post-code lotteries.
The telling satire

of Horace in Tollcross,
as a fellow historian
finding his voice in Scots
called himself, you found

to your taste, and
always demanded
the utmost from
Scottish writers.

The lay of the land,
MacDiarmid's you said,
and precious few others,
but then we all knew

you made a show
of hardly liking
any book, or film
Braveheart being

one you did, really
really like, as a truly
entertaining epic, not
history, nor travesty.

If not a nationalist,
you were most sceptical
about UK plc thriving
on free market nihilism

and rigged bonuses.
You scorned Bush's bile,
and Blair's mendacity,
but kept your respect

for Brown's integrity,
your former student
who paid you a visit
in your final days.

Such was your life,
as it touched one friend,
in a time all too far gone,
the storm on its way.

SIEGFRIED

What drives a man
to drink himself to death
all alone in a dark,
dilapidated flat, trapped
in a coastal town,
its shipyards derelict?

The answer, my friend,
lies in his love of Wagner:
think of him as Siegfried,
a hero forced to always deal
with underlings, so petty
they wore him down.

Angus Calder
1942-2008

TALKING ABOUT GULLS

In memoriam Angus Calder

You seemed
just like Hamlet
warning Guildenstern:
'You would pluck out
the heart of my mystery;'
alert, I could see,
to every trick.

So did we talk
about gulls instead,
who screeched above
for morsels galore,
which they pecked
to nothing.

And so did we sit,
warmed by the sun,
drinking coffee:
two solitudes.

Yet we both knew
that history begins
and ends with how we
relate to one another,
an axiom Horatio
learned from Hamlet,
and that the past is
always present, or
the gulls always
there, as you lit up
a cigarette, looking
at the sky, smoking,
but not oblivious
to Festival crowds

coming in and out from
The Hub in Edinburgh,
the Castle ramparts
so near, that cloudy,
windy day in August.

VI

Christ taught: love your brother
as yourself, but don't forget –
you're one thing, he's another.

from 'Proverbs and Little Songs'

Antonio Machado

(translated by Don Paterson)

THE PIANIST
        for Donny O'Rourke

Just recall
a Polish pianist
playing Chopin
for the SS.

What agonies
he must endure,
and lucky escapes,
in Polanski's film.

It's quite a story
of helpless survival
suddenly interrupted
in medias res:
first, by brands to sell,
then the News.

Our priorities
must be right,
if you think about it,
and keep in mind
such a dark time:
you, or your neighbour,
could be sporting
a yellow star,
or rounded up
to be tattooed.

Now, all they do
is remind you
that you're worth it.

But hey, we're free
to be affronted,
or merely bored.
Put the kettle on.

After all, a film
is just a film,
let's face it.

GREAT WAR POKER

Start with the Kaiser,
he's the strongest card.
In the flamboyant
portrait by August Bocher,
his imperious moustache
so much his trademark,
he faces us squarely,
right hand on his hip,
left hand clutching gloves
and his ceremonial sword:
it's clear he craves to be
a noble warrior, complete
with a golden sash across
his blue-jacketed uniform.

Field-Marshall Haig
is his nemesis, Orpen's
portrait appears to reveal,
with its dash of red adorning
his collar, and colourful,
thin service ribbon bars
above his left jacket pocket.
As he faces us with a hint
of stolidly stubborn
determination, his bearing
tells us he'll soon turn
to leave, yet to his back
is a miasma of uncertainty.

Baron von Richthofen
is an ace of a different
kind, killer in the skies
above countless miles
and mazes of trenches
on the Western Front.
His photograph,
cap tilted at an angle,

is evidently an official
pose, shadow to the left
side of his face, collar
upturned, the 'Pour Le
Merit' medal proudly
hanging from his neck.

Unlike Haig setting off
for battle headquarters,
Orpen's Churchill
seems to be descending,
on the way out. As he faces us,
his civilian face self-reflective,
in the aftermath of Gallipoli.
More casual than the Kaiser's,
his right hand holds his hat,
and his left doesn't need
a sword; an almost loose
bow-tie just keeping
a semblance of elegance
and composure.

Gavrilo Princip, captured
by an Austrian police
mug-shot, wears an ill-
fitting jacket and, it seems,
no shirt underneath:
his sunken eyes, heavy
eyebrows and thin
moustache of a young
Bosnian Serb, make
him look bewildered.
To the left of his face,
a shadowy eclipse
suits such a low,
tragically wild card.

FRANCO AT BAY

Franco did not fall
No one could push him
Saint Theresa he loved
Spaniards he suppressed
Or executed

His conscience, ghostly curses
His prayers, harshly glum
But he did clutch
A rosary, only to simply
Die

ALGIERS, 1943

I couldn't resist
asking Eisenhower,
his smile a wily one,
'Have you talked
to Rommel, that
foxy tactician, after
his surrender?'

 He looked at me,
straight in the eye,
and said, 'I'm here
to kill Germans,
not to talk to them.'
I swear to you,
I felt like an idiot.

'Just a minute,'
you tell me,
'Rommel never
surrendered, fever
seized him, so
he left, returning
to the Reich.'

'Details,' I insist,
'I knew Ike, he was
a son of a bitch,
not like Rommel,
who took cyanide,
to protect his family,
on Hitler's Orders.'

SERMON ON THE MOUND

'And who is my neighbour?' Luke 10:29

a conservative
loves his neighbour
at exclusive times
and ritzy places

a liberal
loves his neighbour
at all times
if like-minded

a nationalist
loves his neighbour
if she talks like him
and lives next door

an internationalist
loves his neighbour
if he pleads for aid
without complaint

a socialist
loves his neighbour
if he's all for equality
and drinking claret

an anarchist
loves his neighbour
in a mystic trance
of utopian promise

a terrorist
can't tell who
is his neighbour
and who isn't

but the earth spins
like a billiard ball
and unseen gamblers
raise the stakes

THE ONLY SPANISH GENERAL IN HAVANA

You have shot
in the back of the neck
an exploiter of claustrophobic mines,
but first you showed him
the jewelled ripples of the expansive ocean
below the sheer, vertiginous cliff.

You have met
Hemingway insanely drunk,
expansive with American bravado,
while shells exploded
in the crowded, cratered streets of Madrid,
just after a Busby Berkeley musical.

As token Anarchist
promoted to a generalship,
you fought off conscripted Moors
to protect a column surrounded by Fascist troops.
'No Pasaran!,' you cried,
and the capital fell.

With the bitter taste of Pernod on your lips,
you watched resentful French reactionaries
beg Hitler for the final blow
as the Germans invaded
through bypassing the Maginot Line.
But you survived the war,
and so did Franco's Spain.

In a clearing
deep in the jungle of Yucatan,
training recruits yet again for the Revolution,
your pent-up nostalgia turned into a liberating
weapon,
and you ripped off all your stripes
to reshape the destinies of an entire continent,
along with Castro, Che Guevara and the guerilleros.

Your reward was to find a wife
and play with Cuban children.
Now your life is like a dream
that's faded. There is nothing
left to face, except that final cliff.

AIR STRIKE

    Benghazi, 2011

1

The outskirts:
tanks like
twisted dragons,
strewn in the desert
smoke and fire
guttering out.

One last screech
fading out of
the sky.

2

'We don't have
a problem
with infidel nations
bombing Gaddafi.

He is an infidel
himself, so why,
since we're good
Muslims, should
we worry about
having other
infidels bomb him?

We're more
than happy
with you infidels
helping us:
it's really Allah
who devastates.'

3

'No, this does not
make me happy.
Do we not call Allah
The Compassionate?

Do not forget,
that these dead,
on their faces
the sun, pitiless
and blinding to us,
are Muslims, and
we are Muslims,
we shall cover
and bury them,
with respect.'

VII

Poetry is a pheasant disappearing in the brush.

from 'Adagia'

Wallace Stevens

STYLE IS THE MAN

To win a Booker, we all agree,
You've got to be stylish, but look,
your style doesn't cut the mustard
like that of another Dickens, or
even Wilde. Sure yours is peppery
and possibly on target, but so shallow
in outlook there's no real story, it's
just the privileged sneer of discontent:
the self obsessed by itself.

RESURRECTION

Spiked
to a crossbeam,
the blood-drained man
stretches out
like yellowed parchment,
ready to crumble into dust,
but for golden scrolls
which crisply document
his disappearance,
as He predicted.

KINGDOMS OF THE MIND

for John Manson

It was Alistair Cooke
who said, 'The American
South is one of those
kingdoms of the mind,
like India or Scotland,
that is neat and easy
to understand only
to people who have
never been there.'

But consider the caste
system in India, so easy
to understand: it's just
a stricter way of casting
out *losers* and rewarding
winners. That's all there is
to it. And if the *Taj Mahal*
is so romantic, the *Kama
Sutra* has its own allure.

Tartan Week in New York
celebrates chivalric sympathy
for defeated Highlanders,
a sentiment not unknown
to the *Ku Klux Klan* defeated
at Reconstruction, only to be
reborn as the White Furies
in *The Birth of a* Nation,
D.W. Griffith's insidious epic.

Both Scotland and India
Cooke found much too foreign,
and the South remote from
New York; as the Abolitionists

knew, a distorted version
of the American Dream,
or a nightmare kingdom,
in which to follow the worst
impulses of our nature.

DRAGON FRUIT

for Andrew Forster

It's right here,
not like Yorick's skull,
but so much nicer
to contemplate.

I take it in my hand,
and it's snug to handle
but it looks like
a small pineapple,

or like a hand-grenade:
this one is from Vietnam
and how can one
forget that war?

It's actually a cactus
pollinated by moths,
hence deemed *Lady
of the Night.*

Look again, it's
red and scaly,
soft to the touch,
thus ready to eat.

Is it really like
a cross between
a puffer fish and
Venus fly- trap?

So one gourmet
has described it,
such flamboyant
flourish like Neruda's.

Yet he never wrote
an elemental ode
to this fruit, so
medicinal in value,

reputed to lower
blood-pressure
and boost protein.
Sweetly bland

to the taste, it
testifies to the
birth of a world
breaking free

from monopolies
of banana or cocoa,
the pitaya its humbler,
less exotic name.

Sliced in half,
it's not like a cranial
cavity, but a universe
of countless seeds.

SOAP

It's not
a laughing
matter.

*And you,
You're doing
my head in!*

I can't turn
the clock
back!

*Sorry, I can't
get my head
round it.*

But you've
got to hear
me out.

*No way,
why should I,
tell me?*

How about
a bacon
butty?

*Forget it,
I can't forgive,
nor forget.*

RAVEL'S WALTZ

Ravel's *La Valse*,
like a discordant dance
macabre, stops abruptly,
so did his own life
due to a brain tumor
which simply wasn't
there, the operation
via local anaesthetic,
superfluous.

What's the point?
Ravel's *Waltz* insists
on telling us, but the
point is in the dance,
a dance to the music
of time, time never
to be regained, or his
version of *Let's Face
the Music and Dance*.

1879 Wallace Stevens 1955

WORDS OF THE FRAGRANT PORTALS, DIMLY-STARRED,
AND OF OURSELVES AND OF OUR ORIGINS,
IN GHOSTLIER DEMARCATIONS, KEENER SOUNDS.

HARTFORD HARMONIUM

It's just a postcard of a Hartford,
Connecticut city view from Bushnell
Park: a glimpse of the Civil War Memorial
Arch behind a tree resplendent
in green, tinged by autumnal gold.

An isolated church-steeple
points to a blue sky, and placid
white clouds. But dominant
Lego-like Insurance Company
buildings seem to mock the spire,

sharp as a bayonet: a view
that Wallace Stevens himself
possibly found monotonous; his
poems, hosannas to a life of
dedicated, irreverent perception.

EPILOGUE

Listen. Each grace note steps in place.
There are no fragments in our universe.

from 'Genesis'

G.F. Dutton

NEWTON'S GOD

'May God us keep
From Single vision
& Newton's sleep.'

So said William
Blake, but Newton's
vision shone

like a bright star
when he wrote
his commentary

on *Revelation*,
combining science
and technology:

'If you eat an apple
which fell on your head,'
Newton said, 'it sets

you thinking,
why it falls always
the same way

that everything
falls, isn't that
the secret force

God hath devised
to keep the sun
and the moon,

constellations
entire, in majestic
motion?

And it will be so
to the end of time,
so St. John's dream

is totally correct,
the Four Horsemen
will cry havoc

and devastate,
but they'll come,
and assuredly go.

Death excepted,
which can't be helped,
we must accept it.

It's the way I see it,
not some puffed-up,
apocalyptic cleric.

All shall still be well,
we must not be afraid
to decipher the silence

of infinite space.
I submit that science
is only the servant

of prophecy, it's
a quest for insight
we find so dazzling,

that where once
we were blind, we
can all now see.'

Pope had it right:
'Let Newton be,
and all was light.'

Notes on the Poems

Saint Francis

This poem was first published in *Chapman*, in the double issue no. 100-101 (2002), edited by Joy Hendry.

Cormorant

This poem was first published in *Southlight 12* (Autumn 2012), together with 'Gauguin' and 'Dragon Fruit'.

Bukowski's Sparrows

This poem was first published in *Southlight 15* (Spring 2014), together with 'Heartache'. It is dedicated to Ronnie Jack.

Magpie

This poem is dedicated to Anita and Myles Shanley.

A Fleet of Mallards

This poem is dedicated to Clem and Chris Seecharan.

Jubilee 2012

This poem was first published in *Fras 18* (2013). It is dedicated to David Dabydeen.

Caruso

This poem was first published in *The Antigonish Review*, no. 177 (Spring 2014).

Old Pontiac: Rawdon Rapids, Quebec

This poem is dedicated to my brother Joe and his wife Jo-Anne, who live in Sydney, Australia.

Mr Hood

This poem is dedicated to my Australian nephews, Joe and Javier, and Jinnez, my niece.

Isaac Bashevis Singer

Isaac Bashevis Singer (1902-1991) was awarded the Nobel Prize for Literature in 1978. The poem was first published in *The Antigonish Review*, no. 177 (Spring 2014). The poem is dedicated to Graham Sutton.

The Pocket-Diary

The late David Pirnie, who passed away in February 2014, ran his own Arts consultancy with immense dedication, and shrewd judgements about practical ways in which culture and the Arts can flourish. His assistance and advice were widely appreciated, particularly by Scottish PEN and the Scottish Poetry Library. The poem is dedicated to Sue Pirnie.

A Newgate Portrait

William Hogarth's *Portrait of Sarah Malcolm* can be seen in the National Gallery of Scotland. It is exhibited with the following information: 'Sarah Malcolm was executed at the age of 25 for the murder of her mistress Lydia Duncombe in 1733. She is seen in Newgate Prison where she sat for Hogarth two days before her execution on 7 March.' The poem first appeared in *Markings*, no.26 (2008).

John Grierson

The poem is about the pioneering Scottish documentary filmmaker and theorist John Grierson (1898-1972). He was born near Stirling. Among many other documentaries, he directed *Drifters* (1929), which was originally screened with Eisenstein's *Battleship Potemkin*, and produced *Night Mail* (1936), famous for its voice-over poem of the same title by W.H. Auden. In 1968, he lectured on film at McGill University, where he screened what he regarded to be the most significant films of the twentieth century.

Art Critic

The poem was inspired by a visit to the Tate Modern exhibition of Paul Klee's paintings in March 2014.

Philosopher on Safari

This poem was published in *Lines Review* no. 83 (June 1985), when the journal was edited by Trevor Royle, to whom the poem is dedicated. 'Words and Looks' was published in the same issue.

Covenant

An earlier version of this poem was published in *Markings*, no.14 (2002).

A Good Man

Dr John Brown taught Modern British History at the University of Edinburgh. His book on *The British Welfare State* came out in 1995. Angus Calder published *Horace in Tollcross*, his contemporary Scots version of the Roman satirist, in 2000. The poem is dedicated to Geraldine Brown. It was first published in *Fras 17* (2012).

Talking About Gulls

Angus Calder was a historian, essayist and poet who harked back to the Enlightenment in his intellectual curiosity, which was so distinctive in works like *The People's War*, *The Myth of the Blitz*, and *Revolutionary Empire*, but also in collections of essays, like *Scotlands of the Mind*, and books of literary criticism, such as *Russia Discovered*, a very fine critical study of Russian writers, politics and culture from Pushkin to Chekhov, and a classic of its kind. Earlier versions of this poem were published in *For Angus* (2009), ed. by Richard Berengarten and Gideon Calder, and in *Fras 18* (2013), edited by William Hershaw and Walter Perrie.

The Pianist

This poem was first published in *Northwords Now,* issue 19 (Autumn/Winter 2011), p. 18.

Great War Poker

The poem resulted from a visit to an exhibition of 'The Great War in Portraits' at the National Portrait Gallery, London in May 2014.

Franco at Bay

This poem was first published in *Poetry Scotland*, no.18 (2001), edited by Sally Evans.

Algiers, 1943

This poem was suggested by an interview with George Stevens in Patrick McGilligan's *Film Crazy: Interviews with Hollywood Film Legends* (2000).

Sermon on the Mound

This poem, written long before Mrs Thatcher's address to the General Assembly of the Church of Scotland, is dedicated to my first wife, Catherine Burns Relich (1937-1983), as it attempts to capture her own nuanced views about the politics at the time. She was a Classics teacher. I met her in Montreal, at a school where she taught Latin, although her first love was the language and civilisation of the ancient Greeks. It was Cathy, Scottish in a European-minded way, who first introduced me to Edinburgh and its history as 'The Heart of Mid-Lothian'. An earlier version of the poem appeared in *Scottish Writing* (Autumn 1974), published by BBC Radio 4 VHF, and edited by Donald Campbell.

The Only Spanish General in Havana

This is a revised version of a poem which first appeared in *Seven New Voices* (Garret Arts, 1972). Among the other poets were Liz Lochhead, Andrew Greig, and Brian McCabe. The book was published and edited by Edinburgh University student impresario at the time, John Schofield. The poem is dedicated to David Walls, who was also a contributor.

Air Strike

This poem is based on newspaper and television reports of the West's and NATO's intervention to assist Libyan rebels in the civil war to overthrow the dictator Muammar Gaddafi in March 2011.

Style is the Man

The title of the poem alludes to a dictum by the French critic Charles Augustin Sainte-Beuve, who was much admired by Matthew Arnold – but hated by Marcel Proust.

Resurrection

This poem first appeared in *LITTACK*, vol.2 no.3 (August 1974), edited by William Oxley.

Hartford Harmonium

This poem, together with 'Soap', was first published in *The Interpreter's House*, no. 48 (2011). It is dedicated to Ron Butlin and Regi Claire.

ABOUT THE POET

Born in Zagreb, Mario Relich grew up in Montreal, Canada, where he obtained his MA in English Literature from McGill University. He did his post-graduate studies at Edinburgh University, leading to a Ph.D. thesis on philosophical dialogue during the Enlightenment, and has lived in Edinburgh most of his life. His parents – Canadian citizens – were originally from Croatia and Italy.

He has been an Associate Lecturer in English Literature and Film Studies at the Open University in Scotland for many years, which led to his involvement as a member of the Open History Society in Scotland, latterly as committee chairman. He has also taught at the Edinburgh College of Art, Napier University, and the University of Ife, Nigeria.

He has contributed articles and reviews to, among other publications, *Scottish Affairs*, *Lines Review*, *Scottish Review of Books*, *West Africa*, and to *The Scotsman*, for which he did theatre reviews when Allen Wright was Arts Editor. His interview with Iain Crichton Smith was published in *Edinburgh Review*, and his articles on Sharon Olds and the American critic and poet Adam Kirsch in *The Dark Horse*. He contributed essays on Hamish Henderson for *At Hame Wi' Freedom: Essays on Hamish Henderson* (Grace Note Publications, 2012) and on Alexander Trocchi for *View from Zollernblick: Regional Perspectives in Europe* (Grace Note Publications, 2013). His essay on Robert Lowell and other poet-translators of Baudelaire was published in *Critical Insights: The Poetry of Baudelaire*, edited by Tom Hubbard (Salem Press, Grey House Publishing, 2014).

He began writing poems in Canada, an interest which was reinforced by attending Robert Garioch's sessions on Scottish poetry when the poet was Writer-in-Residence at the University of Edinburgh. His poems have been published in various periodicals over the years, and this is his first collection. He is also Secretary of the Poetry Association of Scotland and a member of the executive committee of Scottish PEN.

ABOUT THE ARTIST

TOM HUBBARD is mainly a novelist and poet whose second novel, *The Lucky Charm of Major Bessop*, has just been published by Grace Note. He recently edited a book of essays, *The Poetry of Baudelaire* (New York: Grey House), to which Mario Relich contributed an essay on translations of the French poet. Tom has been a visiting professor at various universities in Europe and the USA, and was the first librarian of the Scottish Poetry Library. Just as Mario has now revealed himself as a poet, Tom's secret as wielder of pencil, chalk and charcoal is now out, after long years of reticence on that front. He is also a Fifer, but that was only too obvious from the beginning.

Tom would like to thank Jamie Reid-Baxter who suggested the drawings in this collection.

Made in the USA
Charleston, SC
22 November 2014